Positive Publications
AF578415
12 Rhymes of Christmas
A collection of festive poetry
By #Hatman

Written and Illustrated
by
Martyn James Gordon Ware

contact@hatman.co.uk
www.hatman.co.uk

ISBN: 9798366239233

TABLE OF CONTENTS

Turn On The Lights	2
Saint Nick	4
The Naughty Elf	6
Christmas Cards	8
Christmas Jumper Time	10
Christmas Advent	12
Christmas Shopping	14
Christmas Crackers	16
Christmas Tree	18
Winter Solstice	20
Christmas Carols	22
Christmas Wrapping	24
Christmas Chaos	26
To My...This Xmas	28
New Year is Here	30

TURN ON THE LIGHTS

BY #HATMAN

TURN ON THE LIGHTS

Turn on the lights it's Christmas time.
Turn on the lights is the name of this rhyme.

Turn on the lights high and low.
Turn on the lights, let's see them glow.

Turn on the lights on the Christmas tree.
Turn on the light to spread happiness and
glee.

Turn on the lights hanging off the windows.
Turn on the lights so they twinkle when it
snows.

Turn on the lights on Santa's sleigh.
Turn on the lights on the Christmas display.

Turn on the lights on Father Christmas's hat.
Turn on the lights on the roof and door mat.

Turn on the lights to brighten up the night
sky's
Turn on the lights to bring joy to our eyes.

SAINT NICK

СВЕТИ
НИКОЛА

BY #HATMAN

SAINT NICK

A man of generosity, a heart of gold
He kept on giving until he was old
He gave to the needy, he gave to the poor
He left coins in people's boots left on the floor
His charity work made him a Saint of children and sailors
He helped everyone from pawnbrokers to tailors.
He dedicated his life to those sickly and suffering
He left money in shoes which could probably do with a buffering.

St Nicholas translates to the "People's Victory"
This was a man that thought more about the "we".
His dedication to providing help to those in need.
Has started a trend that has planted a seed.

Today we buy gifts for each other and eat lots of food.
To forget about others is simply just rude.
So be a saint and do good for another.
Give a gift to the poor, not just your lover.

St Nick was the saint that inspired Santa Clause
In this world of karma we must respect it's laws.
Be good and do good, may good come to you.
St Nick paved the way but there's still lots to do.

THE NAUGHTY ELF

BY #HATMAN

THE NAUGHTY ELF

The naughty Elf is watching
While the children play
The naughty Elf is listening
Be careful what you say

The naughty Elf is spying
Making sure you go to sleep
The naughty Elf is laying
Making sure the promises you keep

The naughty Elf is sitting
While you work at school
The naughty Elf is swinging
Checking that your not playing the fool

The naughty Elf is smiling
As a child reads their book
The naughty Elf is laughing
As the boy helps daddy cook

The naughty Elf is flying
Back to Santa's den
The naughty Elf sleeping
But he will be back again.

CHRISTMAS CARDS

BY #HATMAN

CHRISTMAS CARDS

Children's make Christmas cards to send to their pals
Some have penguins others have owls

There's some long ones and thin ones and tiny ones too.
Some have Santa sitting on the loo.

We have dinosaurs and hamsters dressed up as elves
Pictures of the Nativity sitting on our shelves.

There are all different animals with Christmas hats on their heads
Some cards are green but most of them red

There are round ones and square ones
But most are oblong
Some have written inside the words to a song

Some have poems with words that delight
Some are just empty waiting for you to write.

There are those that sparkle and those that pop out
And some share the message of what Christmas is about.

CHRISTMAS JUMPER TIME

BY #HATMAM

CHRISTMAS JUMPER TIME

It's that time of the year
When Christmas jumpers start to appear.

Red ones, green ones and some lime
Some have trees on others pines

Striped ones, spotty ones and plain ones too.
What Christmas jumper defines you?

Reindeers, snowmen and some with snowflakes
Some have patterns and funny shapes.

Funny ones, silly ones, some just rude.
Some are simple, others crude.

There are ones with Santa flying on his sleigh.
Others have elf's playing on Christmas day

There's ones with lights that flash in the dark.
There are others with Santa as a baby shark.

There are others with sequins that change how they look.
Some have characters from your favourite book.

Some are based on films or children's cartoons.
Some have Santa flying over the moon.

These jumpers are as crazy as the people underneath.
I think when Christmas is over
We all breathe a sigh of relief.

CHRISTMAS ADVENT

25

23 24

19 20 21 22

14 15 16 17 18

8 9 10 11 12 13

1 2 3 4 5 6 7

BY #HATMAN

CHRISTMAS ADVENT

It marks the countdown to Christmas.
It's that time of the year.
Each door that is opened tells us Xmas is near.

Behind each opening a surprise awaits
The humble beginnings of the advent states...

People would mark off the days with chalk
Or by lighting a candle while religious lessons were taught.

They originated in Germany just like the Christmas tree
But the great war brought the idea to its knees.

They came back to the fore with chocolate gifts inside.
Counting down until the big day arrives.

CHRISTMAS SHOPPING

BY #HATMAM

CHRISTMAS SHOPPING

Christmas Shopping.
Christmas shopping 12 days to go
Got to buy presents for everyone I know

Something for Mum
Aunty and nanny too.
Let's not forget about cousin John and his motley crew.

My list keeps getting longer, as my credit card takes a hit.
Shopping at Christmas really is shit!

Fighting with the crowds. moving with the herds.
Why do we do it? It's very absurd.

Here for today gone for tomorrow.
All I we keep doing is borrow and borrow.

Christmas shopping, I know it's only once a year.
But aren't we meant to be celebrating not living in fear

Will she like it? Have I got the right size?
I see she hates it, I can tell by her eyes.

It's no surprise the internet has taken over
As who wants all this stress
Christmas should be simple but now it's a mess....

CHRISTMAS CRACKERS
BY #HATMAN

CHRISTMAS CRACKERS

Paper crackers , Shiny crackers
Even very tiny crackers.
You have blue ones and red ones
Budget and luxury ones.

The poppers and the snappers
The pullers and the holders
The jokes for the olders.

The small toys, the paper hats
The magic tricks,
Frogs doing acrobats.

The bangs the oohs,
Who wins who lose.

A Christmas without crackers,
Would be crackers in itself.

Time to get them down,
off the top shelf.

CHRISTMAS TREE

BY #HATMAN

CHRISTMAS TREE

The Christmas tree is shining bright
Decorated with barbells and flashing lights.

Sparkled with glitter and hanging star's
Presents underneath from dolls to toy cars.

The angle flashing at the top of the tree
Her sequins glittering for all to see

The aroma of Christmas is in the air
The pine leaves are falling everywhere.

From tall ones to short ones they represent that the festive season is here
The countdown has started and the big day is near.

The Christmas tree brings happiness and hope
One day it will grow tall and strong like an oak.

The evergreen is a symbol of eternal life
Gifts for everyone from husband to wife.

Ancient traditions are carried on to this day.
The tree is a sign better times are on their way.

WINTER SOLSTICE

BY #HATMAN

WINTER SOLSTICE

They mark it with fire and light
For the winter solstice has the fewest hours of daylight.

Solstice comes from the Latin word sun and stand still.
It's on this day many would kill.

As a sacrifice to the gods to bring back the sun,
As this day signifies a new year has begun.

From the lighting of logs to decorating of trees.
The winter solstice has so many similarities.

From the debauchery of Rome to Christmas parties back home.
These pagan traditions seem to have been cloned.

Around the world from Mexico to Japan,
they give thanks to the sun gods by lighting fires across the land.

From the Yin to the Yang the solstice represents the the change of the season
With days becoming longer as the earth tilts is the reason.

Sun gods to Saints promise of a brighter tomorrow in their stories.
Stone age monuments capture the sunrise in all its glory.

The history of the solstice teaches us this..
In days of darkness we should treat them with bliss.

As tomorrow represents a new day in time
Things can only get better as each day is divine.

CHRISTMAS CAROLS
BY #HATMAN
Silent Night! Holy Night!
Joseph Mohr, 1818
Trans. by John F. Young, 1863
... found Mary, and Joseph, and the babe lying in a manger.
1. What Child is this, who, laid
All Ye Faithful
... even unto Bethlehem ... Luke 2:15
ADESTE FIDELES Irreg. Ref.
John F. Wade's Cantus Diversi, 1751
Angels We Have
Glory to God in the highest and on earth
French carol
Phillips Brooks, 1868
Thou, Bethlehem ...
O Littl

CHRISTMAS CAROLS

On a bleak winter's night
In royal David city a little donkey walked into
the little town of Bethlehem

Whilst Shepherds watched their flocks
Away in a manger
Mary's boy child was born who would bring
Joy to the world

On this holy night
Three kings would come
as they had heard the herald angels sing,
they would bring
gifts of Frankincense and mirr

They were joined by a Sheppard playing a pipe
As a star shone above on this silent night
This was the first Noel
As the Angel Gabriel message told Mary
To come, all ye faithful.
As Snow fell on this white Christmas.

CHRISTMAS WRAPPING

BY #HATMAN

CHRISTMAS WRAPPING

It's almost time for Christmas,
and the presents still need to be wrapped.
We must get them from their hiding place,
and get them all unpacked.

Then comes the process of wrapping,
with paper and scissors in tow.
Not forgetting the ribbon name tags,
nor the fancy coloured bow.

The wrapping paper needs to be chosen,
to reflect who the gift is for.
Will it be the parcels in Santa's sleigh,
or the Holly patterned one on the floor?

To wrap each gift is a special skill in itself.
It is known to be hazardous even bad for your health.
Some do it on the table, others on the ironing board.
Others just put their gifts in bags which is the biggest fraud.

How ever you choose to do it,
the opening is the favourite part.
As we get to rip open the paper,
whilst tearing it all apart.

So all the thought and time that goes into making the gifts look pretty.
Is quickly thrown in the bin,
which is such a pity.

So next time you open a gift,
think about the effort that's gone in.
Before you rip off the paper,
then throw it in the bin.

CHRISTMAS CHAOS

BY #HATMAN

CHRISTMAS CHAOS

The big day is here
Santa has arrived
We got through the build up
How did we survive?

We been up all night
Wrapping the last of the presents
Preparing the food from turkey to pheasants.

At the crack of dawn children wake us from our slumber
Wanting to open their presents that are under..

The Christmas tree that is bursting to the brim
The kiddies can't wait to get stuck in.

Taking turns to play Santa, the pressies are all dished out.
The opening commences which soon becomes a rout.

With paper flying everywhere, yay's and yips add to the sound.
A massive pile of wrapping paper is left upon the ground.

The gifting storm is over as the children sit quietly content.
But a darling auntie seems to be intent.

In causing further chaos by supplying sugary snacks.
After the consumption of these delights, the kids are back on the attack..

Screams and groans soon follow
As do tears of pain.
All this Christmas chaos is really starting to drain.

What little enthusiasm I had, at the start of the day.
A quick nap soon follows and everything is ok.

TO MY...THIS XMAS
BY #HATMAM

TO MY ..THIS XMAS

To my new ones
My old ones

To my future ones
My past ones

To my big ones
my small one

To my close ones
and the far ones

I wish you all
Big love and small kisses

On this festive day
You have all helped on this journey
to this very day

So enjoy this time together
Whether your far or near
Wishing you a merry Xmas
Spreading the Christmas cheer

NEW YEAR IS HERE

BY #HATMAN

NEW YEAR IS HERE

Bang bang,
There goes another year
As the fireworks go up
The crowds cheer

Splashed across the sky's colours bloom
As the fireworks boom
Fizz goes the rockets as they fly through the air
Down below the noise pounds from the fair

Pop goes the poppers as the streamers fall to the floor
Ching goes the glasses of those rich and those poor

Honk goes the horns to bring in a new year
As the sky's sparkle with promise and cheer

It's time to reach out to those far and those near
Time to celebrate as a new year is here.

ABOUT ME

Hatman, poet, performer and children's book writer. Born in 1975, raised in London, England. Hatman's writing talent was first discovered at the age of 7 when he won his first class poetry competition. He has since gone on to write and perform in schools, colleges and on the London poetry scene over the last 30 years.

As a dyslexic author, Hatman provides inspiration to to children and adults with his Positive Poetry which he aims to #InspireHumanity

Visit
www.hatman.co.uk

www.ingramcontent.com/pod-product-compliance
Lightning Source LLC
LaVergne TN
LVHW010510160826
845677LV00012B/2779
9798366239233